AFRICAN TRADITIONAL RELIGION
AND
THE CHRISTIAN FAITH

TITLES ISSUED

1. Tite Tiénou, *The Theological Task of the Church in Africa*
2. Byang Kato, *Biblical Christianity in Africa*
3. Gottfried Osei-Mensah, *Wanted: Servant Leaders*
4. Cornelius Olowola, *African Traditional Religion and the Christian Faith*
5. Osadoler Imasogie, *Guidelines for Christian Theology in Africa*

Theological Perspectives in Africa: No. 4

AFRICAN TRADITIONAL RELIGION AND THE CHRISTIAN FAITH

Cornelius Olowola, BTh, ThM, ThD

1993

AFRICA CHRISTIAN PRESS

© AFRICA CHRISTIAN PRESS
First Edition 1993

ALL RIGHTS RESERVED

ISBN 9964 - 87 - 798 - 6

Theological Perspectives in Africa

A series of monographs designed to provide, in handy format, theological perspectives on vital issues facing Christianity in Africa today.

General Editor
Tite Tiénou
(Burkina Faso)

Consulting Editors
Gottfried Osei- Mensah (Ghana)
Cornelius Olowola (Nigeria)

Cover Design
Joshua Adjabeng (Ghana)

Trade orders to:
Nigeria: Scripture Union, Oyo Road, P O Box 4011, UIPO, Ibadan
Kenya: Keswick Bookshop, PO Box 10242, Nairobi
Zambia: PO Box 21689, Kitwe
S. Africa: SUPA, 83 Campground Road, Rondebosch 7700
Zimbabwe: Books for Africa Publishing House, PO Box 3471, Harare
Australia: Bookhouse, PO box 115, Flemington Markets, NSW 2129
UK: ACP, 50 Loxwood Ave, Worthing, W. Sussex BN14 7RA

All other orders to:
ACP, PO BOX 30, ACHIMOTA, GHANA, W. AFRICA

CONTENTS

Chapter 1 Introduction 7

Chapter 2 African Beliefs about God 10
    The African concept of God
    The characteristics of God
    Creation myths

Chapter 3 Sources of African Knowledge about God 21
    Africans know God through intuition
    African know God through traditions
    Africans know about God through general revelation
    Africans can know about God through special revelation

Chapter 4 African Beliefs about the Spirit World 30
    The reality of the spirit world
    The origin of spirits in African belief
    Different types of spirits

Chapter 5 Worship of the Spirits 38
    Christianity and spirit worship
    Monotheism or polytheism in African religion
    Christian worship of God

Chapter 6 African Beliefs about Sacrifice 47
    The purpose of African sacrifice
    The contents of African sacrifice
    Those to whom African sacrifice is offered

Chapter 7 Sacrifice in Biblical Perspective 54
    Comparisons between African and Israelite sacrifices
    Sacrifice in the New Testament

Chapter 8 Conclusion 63

Bibliography 66

The views expressed in these monographs are those of each author and do not necessarily represent the views either of the editors of this series or of the publisher.

Chapter One

Introduction

The continuing revival of traditional African religiosity in our day presents a great and unavoidable challenge to Christianity in Africa. Traditional religion is increasingly being taught in secondary school alongside the study of Christianity and Islam. Religious relativism is being promoted by leading scholars of African religion, under the guise of 'religious tolerance'. African traditional religion has established itself in non-African countries like Brazil and Cuba. A growing body of literature has emerged on Africa's traditional religion, produced both by African and by Western scholars. And while Africans are being exposed today to Western education, traditional thought is still the source of the basic world-view of most of the people. The growing Christian population is certainly not exempt from such influences. In our day Christianity in Africa faces traditional religion as never before.

These factors alone give adequate justification why African Christians today must renew their attention to African traditional religion, especially those training in Bible colleges and seminaries, and those studying in secondary schools and universities.

The purpose of this book is to provide a constructive critical approach to African traditional religion from the standpoint of Christian faith. In the past the majority of works on the religious beliefs of Africans were written by non-Africans, and many contained ignorant and derogatory criticisms which have been rightly rejected by Africans. More recently, books on traditional religion have usually been written by African scholars, who for their part have often been uncritically zealous in defending the African religious system. What Christianity in Africa now requires more than ever are studies by African writers which provide a fair and accurate presentation of African traditional religion, together with a critical evaluation in the light of the revealed Word of God, the Bible.

I have attempted to provide such an approach in this book, at an introductory level. My hope is that this material may prove useful as a supplementary text for those studying African traditional religion in the Bible colleges and seminaries of Africa. I hope that it will also prove helpful to Christians studying traditional religion in Africa's secondary schools and universities.

Given the purpose of this book, I have not attempted a comprehensive presentation of African traditional religion. Rather I wish to offer a general sketch, by giving attention to principal elements of African cosmology, namely: (i) God, (ii) the spirits, and (iii) sacrifice. God is seen in traditional religion as the Creator, the spirits are understood as His agents, and man in traditional religion must relate properly to this supernatural order by means including sacrifice. For explanation and illustration I will use one particular example of African traditional religion, namely the religious beliefs and practices of the Yoruba peoples of southwestern Nigeria.

The noted African scholar Awolalu gives six fundamental beliefs of the Yorubas, which apply generally to most examples of traditional religion throughout Africa, and which set the framework for our study. These six fundamental beliefs of traditional religion are as follows:

(i) that this world was brought into being by the Source of all beings as the Supreme Being;

(ii) that the Supreme Being brought into being a number of divinities and spirits to act as His functionaries in the orderly maintenance of the world;

(iii) that death does not write 'the end' to human life but opens the gate to the hereafter—hence prominence is given to belief in the continuation of life after death;

(iv) that divinities and spirits together with the ancestral spirits are in the supersensible world but are interested in what goes on in the world of man;

(v) that there are mysterious powers or forces in the world and that their presence makes man live in fear;

(vi) that if men and women are to enjoy peace, they would live according to the laid-down directives of the Supreme Being and His agents.[1]

We turn now in the following chapters to discuss the principal components of this belief system in the light of the Christian faith.

NOTES

[1] J.O. Awolalu, *Yoruba Beliefs and Sacrificial Rites*, 22.

Chapter Two

African Beliefs about God

In the past there were those from the West who categorically maintained that Africans have no concept whatsoever of God. One such writer made the sweeping and derogatory statement: 'Before the introduction of a genuine faith and higher standard of culture by the Arabs, the natives had neither political organisation nor, strictly speaking, any religion, nor any industrial development. None but the most primitive instincts determine the lives and conduct of the negroes, who lack every kind of ethical inspiration.'[1] Obviously such a statement results from blind ignorance. On the cultural level a little careful observation would have clearly shown that Africans, prior to the coming of the Arabs, did have an organised society. Their own industries provided tools for farming and hunting, utensils for cooking, and clothes to cover themselves. To describe them as 'lacking every kind of ethical inspiration' is merely crude prejudice, as there exists no people group which totally lacks ethical inspiration. That Africans are deeply religious has always been everywhere evident. The famous comment made many years ago by the German scholar Emil Ludwig to a missionary in Africa, 'How can the untutored African conceive God? Deity is a philosophical concept which savages are incapable of framing,'[2] is today noteworthy only for its absurdity.

The African concept of God

Modern scholarship now recognises that a concept of God as supreme being and creator is virtually universal in traditional Africa. Even so, the descriptions often need clarification and refinement.

In Yoruba tradition the most common name for God is Olorun. In fact Yoruba Christianity commonly uses this name for God, and 'God' is translated by 'Olorun' in the Yoruba Bible. 'Olorun' is a simple compound, with the prefix 'Ol' indicating ownership, and 'orun' meaning 'heaven'. Hence 'Olorun' means the owner of heaven. Farrow rightly comments on 'orun':

> Like the English 'heavens' and the Hebrew Shamim, it is used for the sky as well as for the dwelling-place of the Deity. This title, then, expresses the greatness and majesty of God.[3]

Another name for God among the Yoruba is 'Olodumare'. It is generally taken to denote 'the Almighty One', and is used to translate 'Almighty' in the Yoruba Bible. But both the meaning and the derivation of 'Olodumare' are uncertain. Idowu quotes many hitherto unrecorded songs and proverbs to show the antiquity of the name, and suggests that it was the original name for God, and means 'the origin and ground of all that is.'[4] Fadipe, while acknowledging that the meaning is obscure, offers a detailed analysis and concludes that 'Olodumare' means in part 'Lord of destinies'.[5] Lucas writes that the name means 'the chief or the Exalted One to whom I must go or return.'[6] One is inclined, however, to agree with Awolalu that: 'tradition, as held by the elders among the people, confirms that the name connotes one who has the fullness or superlative greatness; the everlasting majesty upon whom man can depend.'[7]

Other Yoruba names for God include 'Eleda', meaning 'the Creator', the self-existing One and the Source of all things; 'Alaaye', which means 'the living One'; 'Elemii' meaning 'the Giver and Owner of life'; and 'Olojo Oni', meaning 'He who owns and controls today.'

The characteristics of God

The characteristics of God in African belief are not entirely dissimilar from those in Christian belief. For example, the Yoruba people believe that God is omniscient and omnipresent. They describe God as 'Eleti igbo aroye' (He who is ever listening to complaints); 'Arinurode Olumo Okaan' (the One who sees both the inside and the outside of a person); and 'Olorunnikan logborn' (only God is wise). Thus Ray explains:

> When the Yoruba feel they have been wronged but cannot avail themselves of any official means of retribution, they may be advised, according to a well-known proverb, 'to allow Olorun to revenge and stand aside.' For Olorun is 'He who sees both the inside and outside (of men).' He is an all-seeing and all-knowing judge. Hence the Yoruba say, 'Those we cannot catch, we leave in the hands of Olorun.' [8]

When something is missing and a search is conducted for many days without a clue, the Yoruba solution is that 'Ohun ti o pa mo, oju Olorun to' (that which is hidden to people is seen by the eyes of God). The same thought occurs in stories. For example, the story is told of a man and his son who went secretly to another man's farm. The father told his son to give him a sign if the son should see anyone coming. The son realised that this was not his father's farm, and wondered what his father was trying to do. As the father started digging yams, his son gave him a sign that someone was coming. The father looked round and asked his son: 'Who is coming?' The son replied, 'If the kings of the earth do not see you, the King of heaven sees you' (bi oba aiye ko ri o oba oke wo o). Since God sees everything, He is described as One with eyes everywhere (Olojukabiajere).

In Yoruba tradition God is also conceived as omnipotent. He is the one who both proposes and disposes. He is 'oba a se kan ma ku' (the King whose works are perfect). Idowu explains correctly: 'He is the One who set the machinery of the universe in motion. He can bring it, in part or as a whole, to a standstill, and set it going again if need be.' [9] It follows that God is also responsible for man's destiny.

> Equally fundamental is the concept of destiny, which is assigned and maintained by Olorun independently of the moral sphere. Accordingly, the wicked may prosper and the just may suffer, for success and failure ultimately derive from Olorun's predetermined plan, not from human striving.[10]

The Yoruba also think of God as transcendent. He is neither a nature god nor a sky god, but above all creation. Some non-Africans have therefore interpreted Yoruba thinking to suggest that God is also remote. For example, Ray writes:

> In comparison to the orisha [spirits], which are essentially local, cultic, personal, active and vocal, Olorun is universal, noncultic, impersonal, inactive, and silent. His relation to mankind is generally indirect and unilateral; he transcends the ritual mechanisms of mutual reciprocity and exchange. He is not directly involved in man's relation with the gods, but stands above that relation as its ultimate condition or sanction.[11]

In the last century Ellis wrote along similar lines:

> Olorun is considered too distant, or too indifferent to interfere in the affairs of the world. The natives say that he enjoys a life of complete idleness and repose, a blissful condition according to their ideas, and passes his time dozing or sleeping. Since he is too lazy or too indifferent to exercise

any control over earthly affairs, man on his side does not waste time in endeavouring to propitiate him, but reserves his worship and sacrifice for more active agents.[12]

But Yoruba scholars have disputed this assessment. Awolalu states flatly: 'To the Yoruba, God (the Supreme Being) is not remote.'[13] Awolalu bases his argument on the fact that the Yoruba call upon God in everyday life. And Fadipe comments:

> It is true that no sacrifice is offered to Olorun by the orisa-worshipping Yoruba, nor is he the object of any formal ritual worship. Far from Olorun being a distant conception to the people, the average Yoruba uses the name, often in proverbs, in prayers and wishes, in promises, in planning for the future, in attempts to clear himself of accusations, in reminding his opponent of his duty to speak the truth, and the like. Indeed, for all general purposes, it is more natural to invoke the name of Olorun than that of orisa.[14]

One may agree that the transcendence and immanence of God are confusing to the average Yoruba. A man will call upon God but then make sacrifice to spirits. God in Yoruba thinking is real and not remote, but man's relationship with the Supreme Being is not clear because of man's futile imaginations. As the Apostle Paul said, 'For even though they knew God, they did not honour Him as God, or give thanks; but they became futile in their speculations, and their foolish heart was darkened' (Romans 1:21-22).

In Yoruba tradition, God is also understood to be a righteous judge who judges all equally. The judgment of man's character whether rich or poor, big or small, is in his hands. He is described as Oba Adake-da-jo (the King who executes judgment in silence). Idowu points out: 'Although He does not arraign evil-doers before a visible judgment-seat, His judgment is nevertheless sure and inescapable.'[15] On the other hand, a concept of God's holiness is lacking in Yoruba religion. Idowu states: 'Here we must go warily. What can be gathered from our sources about the holiness of Olodumare is only by inference.'[16]

Perhaps holiness is implied in His purity. Hence He is described as Oba Mimo (the pure King), and Oba ti ko leri (the King who is without blemish). Ray's conclusion fits well:

> Olorun therefore exhibits a subtle and paradoxical combination of attributes as part of his transcendent nature. He is both supremely moral and supremely amoral, both an active administrator of justice and an arbitrary determiner of destinies.[17]

Creation myths

God is especially known as the Creator in most African traditional religion. The beliefs in creation are conveyed through myths handed down from generation to generation. African Christians should be familiar with these myths, since they are useful as a starting point for leading African traditionalists to biblical teaching about God.

There are many different creation myths which circulate among African peoples. Two Yoruba creation myths will show that Africans generally believe that the creation of the earth was God's idea. He initiated it and commissioned a messenger to do it.

In the first myth God commissioned Obatala, the Yoruba arch-divinity to do the work of creating the earth. It is not clear in the myth what moved God to think of creating the earth. 'He conceived the idea and at once carried it into effect. He summoned Orisa-nla (or Obatala), the Arch-Divinity, to his presence and charged him with the duty.'[18] Obatala was given a packet of loose earth wrapped in leaves or 'in a snail shell'[19] together with a hen and a pigeon which would help him. Taking the material and the tools he headed for his mission. On arrival, 'he threw the loose earth on a suitable spot on the watery waste.'[20] Immediately, the hen and the pigeon that were given to him by God began 'to spread it out over the surface.'[21] Idowu writes:

The sacred spot where the work began was named Ife—'That which is wide' from the Yoruba word 'fe', meaning 'to be wide'. And that, according to the tradition, was how Ife, the Holy City of the Yoruba, got its name. The prefix 'Ile-' was added much later to signify that it was the original home of all, and to distinguish it from the other towns called Ife which have come into existence as a result of migrations.[22]

When Obatala completed his work he went back to report his accomplishment to God, who immediately commissioned a chameleon to go and inspect the work of creation. Idowu explains that 'the chameleon is sacred to the Yoruba; it is variously described as the messenger of Olodumare or the messenger of Orisa-nla.'[23] There were said to be two reports given by the chameleon. According to the first, the earth was not solid enough but on reinspection it was found to be sufficiently solid and therefore ready for habitation. Obatala was asked to equip the earth and given trees to plant so as to provide food. God sent Orunmila (the Oracle divinity) to accompany him to be his counsellor and advisor. The hen and the pigeon were to multiply and provide food for the people of the earth. In addition, God provided for Obatala 'sixteen persons ready-created'[24] by him to be the first inhabitants of the earth. The work of creation was completed in four days and 'the fifth day was set apart for the worship of the Deity and for rest.'[25] This first myth on creation concludes with the story that, as the inhabitants of the earth multiplied, more water was needed. Obatala appealed to God who provided water by sending rain to the earth.

In the second myth Oduduwa created the solid earth. Obatala was the original divinity commissioned to do this work but he became drunk with palm wine and fell asleep. God expected Obatala to return and report on his work, but he waited in vain and finally asked Oduduwa to go in search of Obatala. Oduduwa, finding Obatala fast asleep as a result of his drunkenness, took the materials given to Obatala and went and created the earth. Idowu writes 'Apparently, Oduduwa's action received the approval of Olodumare because, as the myth has it, he thereby supplanted Orisna-nla (that is Obatala), not only in the honour of being the creator of the solid earth, but also in seniority over all the other divinities.'[26]

As to the creation of man, the Yoruba believe that this was the joint effort of Olodumare and Obatala. Obatala was asked by Olodumare 'to people the earth by fashioning man from pieces of clay.'[27] He was designated 'the creator of human physical features for the future.'[28] 'His allotted duty was thenceforth to mould man's physical form from the dust of the earth.'[29] Obatala became the sculptor-divinity with the sole prerogative 'to make at will human figures perfect or defective, and of whatever colours he wants them to be. The hunchback, the cripple, or the albino, are specially marks of his prerogative or, more often than not, displeasure.' [30] On the other hand, it is Olodumare who gives life to what Obatala has designed. 'The right to give life Olodumare reserved to himself alone for ever. The instruction given to Orisa-nla, therefore, was that when he had completed his own part in the creation of man, he should lock up the lifeless form in a room and leave the place. Olodumare would then come and give breath, thus completing the creation of the human being.'[31]

Myths are one of the main sources for learning about traditional African religious belief and history. They tell people about their origin, migration, lineage and religion. Myths confirm that Africans believe that God exists and that he created the universe and man. A biblical theology for Africans must take into account the knowledge which the people already have.

It would, however, be dangerous to formulate a theology based mainly on African myths. Some African myths arise from the desire of one group to assert their superiority over others. Myths can be misleading, and they often leave many unanswered questions. For example, in the Yoruba creation myths, from where did Olodumare get his packet of loose earth? When, and of what, was the pigeon created? Where did the sixteen people come from? Or how do individuals explain their own existence? 'All these point to the fact that there are noticeable gaps in the creation myth.'[32] According to Awolalu, the gaps are less important, because the main emphasis is 'to explain some essential tradition—mainly to emphasise the important fact that Olodumare is the Creator of heaven and earth and of all beings and things.'[33] While this is true, the problems mentioned remain.

For Christians, traditional African myths like those about creation must be corrected by biblical revelation. For example, while the creation myths imply that the world was created out of pre-existing materials, Genesis teaches: 'In the beginning God created the heavens and the earth' (Genesis 1:1). The universe was created by God from nothing. It is 'neither eternal nor formed out of pre-existing things, nor sprung from necessity, but due to the immediate act of God.'[34] The myths give the impression that God commissioned others to do the work of creation, whereas the Bible clearly teaches that God was the sole creator. By the word of his mouth he created the whole universe. After the creation of the universe God was directly responsible for creating man. According to Genesis 1:27, 'God created man in his own image.' Man was created from 'the dust of the ground, and God breathed into his nostrils the breath of life; and man became a living being' (Genesis 2:7). According to this passage God himself is both the sculptor and the life-giver. The mythical description of Obatala having the sole prerogative to create directly at will whatever type he chooses must be rejected in the light of the biblical passages on the creation of man. Since the creation of the first couple, a child's characteristics are transmitted by parents. Any defect in children is genetical and cannot be attributed to a direct act of God. Finally, the Psalmist declares that children are a gift of the Lord (Psalm 127:3-5). It is not Obatala who gives children but God, who has not delegated that authority or power to anyone else.

NOTES

1. L. Frobenius, *The Voice of Africa* 1:1-2, quoting from a 19th century Berlin newspaper.
2. E.W. Smith, *African Ideas of God*, 1.
3. S.S. Farrow, *Faith, Fancies and Fetich*, 27.
4. E.B. Idowu, *Olodumare: God in Yoruba Belief*, 37.
5. N.A. Fadipe, *The Sociology of the Yoruba*, 281.
6. J.O. Lucas, *The Religion of the Yorubas*, 41.
7. J.O. Awolalu, *Yoruba Beliefs and Sacrificial Rites*, 11.
8. B.C. Ray, *African Religions: Symbol, Ritual and Community*, 58-59.
9. Idowu, *Olodumare*, 42.
10. Ray, 59.
11. Ibid., 57.
12. A.B. Ellis, *The Yoruba-Speaking Peoples of the Slave Coast of Africa*, 36-37.
13. Awolalu, 16.
14. Fadipe, 282.
15. Idowu, *Olodumare*, 42.
16. Ibid., 46.
17. Ray, 59.
18. Idowu, *Olodumare*, 19.
19. Awolalu, 13.
20. Idowu, *Olodumare*, 19.
21. Ray, 43.
22. Idowu, *Olodumare*, 20.
23. Ibid.
24. Awolalu, p13
25. Idowu, *Olodumare*, 20.
26. Ibid., 22.
27. Ray, 43.
28. Idowu, *Olodumare*, 21.
29. Ibid.
30. Ibid.
31. Ibid.

[32] Awolalu, 13.
[33] Ibid., 14.
[34] H.C. Thiessen, *Lectures in Systematic Theology*, 112.

Chapter Three

Sources of African Knowledge about God

African sources of knowledge about God include intuition, traditions, general revelation, and the special revelation brought in the Gospel.

Africans know God through intuition

Intuition is an inherent human function. It is 'confidence or belief which springs immediately from the constitution of the mind.' Knowledge of God exists in the soul before sense experience. Pascal wrote: 'We know the truth through our reason but also through our heart. It is through the latter that we know first principles, and reason, which has nothing to do with it, tries in vain to refute them. Knowledge of the first principles, like space, time, motion, number, is as solid as any derived through reason and it is on such knowledge, coming from the heart and instinct, that reason has to depend and base all its arguments.' This applies equally to intuitive knowledge about God. 'The human mind intuitively grasps the existence of a Power, a Perfection, and a Personality who is primal, uncaused and infinite.'[3] The belief in the existence of God and a future life is everywhere recognised in Africa. 'The lowest tribes have a conscience, fear death, believe in witches, propitiate or frighten away evil fates. Even the fetish worshipper, who calls the stone or the tree a god, shows that he has already the idea of God.'[4] Since Africans are human beings 'created in the image of God and universally illumined by the Logos,'[5] they intuitively recognise the reality of God as a first truth. There is scriptural support for the existence of a rudimentary knowledge of God in every man (cf. John 1:9; 16:6; Genesis 1:1; Acts 17:28), and Africans, like all other peoples, know something of God through their intuition.

Africans know about God through traditions

Before Western education, Africans had methods of educating their children. The methods were informal. Children normally sat around their parents during the evenings when the moon was shining to listen to instruction. On the way to the farm, or while travelling, an African father would tell stories to his children. Most of these stories are myths of creation, conquest and migration. A child's education covers all areas of life from how to be a better farmer to how to cure certain kinds of diseases. Since 'myths are virtually the only source of Yoruba history before the arrival of the Europeans,'[6] they were passed from generation to generation. As Biobaku points out, 'Most African rulers keep professional oral historians at their courts. These men, sometimes with drums and trumpets, chant praise-poems and recite dynastic lists with consummate skill. They are usually carefully trained and their office is nearly always hereditary.'[7] Since informal teaching is given on all areas of life, it follows that whatever parents knew about God was passed to the children through myths.

Africans know about God through general revelation

General revelation is also an important source of African knowledge about God. Africans do not deny the fact of revelation. They assert that God took the initiative in making himself known. As Idowu states:

> It is through the fact of God's revelation—the fact that God does make Himself or his truth known to man—that we have any clue at all to certain fundamental issues of life . . . . We find that in every age and generation there is a direct contact of God with the human soul, the personal awareness of God on the part of man through God's own initiative. What man knows of God, what he discovers about God, comes as a result of this self-disclosure.[8]

Africans know God through observing the created order and, as human beings created in the image of God, they are capable of entering into communication with their Creator. Idowu concludes, 'We can deny this primary revelation only when we rob the created order of its revelatory quality and relieve man of his inherent capability to receive divine communication.'[9]

We turn to Scripture for a full explanation about general revelation. In Psalm 19 the author reflects on the glory of God continually revealed in nature. Silently, in a non-verbal but observable way, God reveals himself to all men everywhere through the things he has made, the created order. Paul speaks of creation as the source by which people of all nations and generations may know God's existence and power. 'For since the creation of the world, his invisible attributes, his eternal power, and his divine nature have been clearly seen, being understood through what has been made, so that they are without excuse' (Romans 1:20). The visible creation, God's handiwork, makes manifest the invisible perfections of God, its Creator. Africans, therefore, cannot claim to lack knowledge of the one true God.

God has revealed himself in other ways besides nature. The term 'general revelation' covers all means by which God reveals himself apart from Christ and the Bible. Man can learn about God not only from the created order, but also through God's providential dealings with man in the past and the present. Frequently the Old Testament refers back to the way God delivered his people from slavery in Egypt and gave them a new beginning. As punishment for forgetting him, he allowed them to again become captives of powerful foreign nations. God is the controller and sustainer of the universe (Colossians 1:17). His giving and withholding of rain and productive seasons is often seen as his way of communicating with those who will listen. Africans experience God in this way as do any other peoples.

Africans know about God through special revelation

General revelation by itself, however, is insufficient for the deepest needs of man. General revelation is sufficient to alert a man to his need of God, but general revelation cannot save man. It is only in the special revelation of God which comes through Jesus Christ and the Bible that a person is enabled to know God and to be in saving fellowship with Him. General revelation is limited and inadequate because it reveals the existence, character, and moral demands of God, but does not show the way to redemptive encounter with God.

Special revelation for its part rests on natural revelation as a building rests on its foundation. Warfield explains:

Without general revelation, special revelation would lack that basis in the fundamental knowledge of God as the mighty and wise, righteous and good, maker and ruler of all things, apart from which the further revelation of this great God's interventions in the world for the salvation of sinners could not be either intelligible, credible, or operative.[10]

The purpose of special revelation is to complete the work of general revelation by meeting the need which general revelation cannot meet. Special revelation has been called 'soteriological revelation'; its purpose is to redeem man through Christ. As Adeyemo has written, 'in special revelation God is always in action, speaking, bringing something entirely new to man, something of which he could have no previous knowledge, and which becomes a real revelation only for him who accepts the object of revelation by a God-given faith.'[11] Or as the writer of Hebrews puts it:

> In the past God spoke to our forefathers through the prophets at many times and in various ways, but in these last days he has spoken to us by his Son, whom he appointed heir of all things, and through whom he made the universe (Hebrews 1:1-2).

And Paul wrote:

> When the time had fully come, God sent his Son, born of a woman, born under the law, to redeem those under law, that we might receive the full rights of sons (Galatians 4:4,5).

Special revelation is contained in the Bible. It is there that we learn the facts about God fully, which general revelation made known only imperfectly and in part. There is some truth in African traditional religion, because of the role of general revelation, but this truth is inadequate for redemption. Since God through Christ has confirmed the Bible to be his infallible Word, all religious beliefs must be brought to the bar of Holy Scripture to be tested. 'The Bible alone is the canon or norm for all truth.'[12]

In considering the vital issue of traditional religion and special revelation, the case of Professor Idowu, former chairman of the Department of Religious Knowledge at the University of Ibadan in Nigeria, is especially instructive. Idowu subsequently became head of the Methodist Church in West Africa. In the late 1950s and early 1960s Idowu called upon Nigerians to embrace Christianity because it was the definitive faith demanding the allegiance of the entire world.[13] He also argued that African Christians must not isolate themselves.

> To speak of an indigenous church is not to ask that every mark of 'foreignness' attaching to her should be removed. For the church to attempt to divest herself completely of all 'foreign' elements is . . . to deny herself of the spiritual tonic which 'the communion of the saints' affords.[14]

Idowu's concern in those days 'was to create an indigenous African church that would be truly free to acknowledge the lordship of the eternal Christ, who alone is preeminent'[15] One must fully agree when he wrote:

> By indigenisation in this context, we mean that the Church in Nigeria should be the Church which affords Nigerians the means of worshipping God as Nigerians; that is, in a way which is compatible with their own spiritual temperament, of singing to the glory of God in their own way, of praying to God and hearing His Holy Word in idiom which is clearly intelligible to them.[16]

But by the 1970s Idowu had changed his mind, and began to extol the virtues of non-Christian African religion. Idowu began to sow the seed of religious pluralism and relativism in Africa, by claiming that God's revelation in nature is sufficient for salvation. The effects of such teaching are seen all over the continent. Idowu now insists that God revealed himself redemptively to the African soul, 'and thus the tribal African ought not to repudiate the rich spiritual heritage God has granted his ancestors in traditional religion.'[17] Demerest states that for Idowu:

Spiritualism, fetishism, ancestor worship, magic, ritual medicine, and other practices are all appropriate responses of the African soul on African soil to the *mysterium tremendum et fascinans*.[18]

And yet Idowu's new position is founded on inconsistency. He scolds Africans for allowing themselves to be dominated by Western thought:

> The African expression of the faith must be shorn of all traces of Western colonial influence. The tragedy of Africa is that it has sold its soul to alien European traditions.[19]

But Idowu's own theological system builds on the foundations laid by Kant, Schleiermacher, and Tillich. He borrows his views of revelation from Brunner, Baillie, and DeWolf. As one writer has rightly said: 'Indeed, if the European elements were excised from Idowu's theology, it would collapse and come to naught.'[20]

Idowu's problem is that he confuses natural *revelation* with natural *religion*. The Bible teaches that God does reveal himself through nature. That is natural revelation. But the Bible also clearly teaches that mankind's natural response to that revelation has been rebellious and sinful. That is natural religion.

> For although they knew God, they neither glorified him as God nor gave thanks to him, but their thinking became futile and their foolish hearts were darkened . . . They exchanged the truth of God for a lie, and worshipped and served created things rather than the Creator (Romans 1:21,25).

In Biblical perspective natural *revelation* is one thing, whereas natural *religion* is something else. All religious responses which we devise for ourselves, by which we avoid giving God the sole allegiance which is His due, are biblically condemned. This applies to every man-made religion, anywhere in the world, and therefore it includes Africa's traditional religion:

Every form of natural religion, whatever label it bears, is an expression of sinful man's refusal to honour the God who has plainly revealed himself through the several modalities of general revelation.[21]

There is truth to be found in African traditional religions, as in other religions of mankind, but the teaching of Scripture is clear that this is not redemptive truth. God has spoken redemptively only in his Son as revealed in Scripture:

Salvation is found in no one else; for there is no other name under heaven given to men by which we must be saved (Acts 4:12).

This applies to Africa, and to its religious heritage, as much as it applies to any other part of the world.

NOTES

[1] L.S. Chafer, *Systematic Theology*, 1: 130- 135.
[2] B. Pascal, *Pensées*, numbers 110, 58.
[3] B.A. Demarest, *General Revelation*, 229.
[4] A.H. Strong, *Systematic Theology*, 67.
[5] Demarest, 228.
[6] P.C. Lloyd, 'Yoruba Myths', 20.
[7] S.O. Biobaku, 'The Use and Interpretation of Myths', 13.
[8] E.B. Idowu, *African Traditional Religion*, 56.
[9] E.B. Idowu, 'God,' 19.
[10] B.B. Warfield, *The Inspiration and Authority of the Bible*, 75.
[11] T. Adeyemo, 'The Doctrine of God in African Traditional Religion', 67-68.
[12] C.C. Ryrie, *A Survey of Bible Doctrine*, 29.
[13] Demarest, 202.
[14] E.B. Idowu, *Towards an Indigenous Church*, 12.
[15] Demarest, 203.
[16] Idowu, *Indigenous Church*, 11.

[17] Demarest, 206.
[18] Ibid., 205-206.
[19] Ibid., 208.
[20] Ibid.
[21] Ibid., 207

Chapter Four

African Beliefs about the Spirit World

Africans believe not only in the existence of a Supreme Being but also in divinities and spirits. According to Farrow, the African 'believes intensely in the spirit-world, and in the possibility of exercising, through spirit-agency, a power that can be exercised by no physical means.'[1] For example, Awolalu writes that the Yoruba 'hold the belief that as the Supreme Being created heaven and earth and all the inhabitants, so also did He bring into being the divinities and spirits . . . to serve his theocratic world.'[2] Evidence for the reality of spirits is apparent, because everywhere you in Africa you will find objects of spirit worship. These objects remind their owners of the reality of the existence of these spirits, whom they worship and to whom they sacrifice, believing these spirits are intermediaries between them and the Supreme Being. To deny the existence of these spirits is to deny the existence of African religion.

The reality of the spirit world

Throughout the Bible it is clearly taught that there is indeed an order of beings above human beings. These spirits are both good and bad. The Bible calls the good spirits 'angels' who are 'ministering spirits sent out to render service for the sake of those who will inherit salvation' (Hebrews 1:14). These created beings have intelligence (1 Peter 1:12), and are innumerable (Hebrews 12:22), but they are not equals of God. They are not eternal, since they are created beings. They served Christ on many occasions, predicting his birth (Luke 1:26-33), protecting and strengthening him at the time of his temptations and crucifixion. They minister also to believers (Acts 12:7) and even to unbelievers (Acts 12:23). The Bible nowhere teaches that angels are intermediaries between God and man. They are God's agents in dealing with men. As such, they are not to be worshipped or propitiated through sacrifices.

The Bible also speaks of evil spirits, called 'demons', who are agents of the devil.

> Actual communication with unseen spirits, their influence on nations, and demon-possession are taught clearly and unmistakably in both the Old and New Testaments. The Bible recognises not only the material world, but a spiritual world intimately connected with it, and spiritual beings both good and bad, who have access to, and influence for good or ill, the world's inhabitants.[3]

Jesus himself dealt with numerous cases of demon possession during his earthly ministry. The effectiveness of Jesus' power to exorcise caused people to marvel and therefore to reflect on who he was. The gospel writers portray Christ not only as one who healed many demon-possessed people but also as one who was frequently accused by his enemies of being demon-possessed himself. In John 7:20, when those who were trying to kill him realised that he knew their plan, they retorted that he must have a demon in him. After healing the man born blind (John 10) there was a sharp difference of opinion among the witnesses, as some concluded he was demon-possessed and others, judging by the evidence rather than their prejudices, admitted that neither his words nor actions were those of a person possessed by a demon. On occasions Jesus confronted people who were allowing themselves to be used as instruments of the devil. Judas and the Pharisees both came into this category. Some of his parables clearly depict the destructive work of the devil.

Africans know that to deny the existence of the devil, evil spirits and demon-possession is to deny reality. I have witnessed demon activities in predominantly non-Christian parts of Nigeria. This is one of the major areas where African traditional beliefs identify more naturally with the biblical world-view than do Western ideas, where scientific knowledge has often led people to categorise belief in spiritual powers as ignorant and superstitious.

The origin of spirits in African belief

Scholars are not in agreement on the origin of spirits or divinities according to African traditional belief. Idowu contends that divinities are derivatives from Deity, spirits who have no beginning and probably no ending. 'It will not be correct to say that divinities were created. It will be correct to say that they were brought into being, or that they came into being in the nature of things with regard to the divine ordering of the universe.'[4] According to Idowu, Orisa-nla (arch-divinity among the Yoruba) is definitely a 'derivation partaking of the very nature and metaphysical attributes of Olodumare.'[5]

But other scholars are not so sure. Farrow points to diverse origins, 'Some of them, according to the mythology of the country, were always spirits, of divine origin, existing prior to all creation; others are deified men; others again are the spirits of animals, trees, rocks etc.'[6] Fadipe denies the concept of divine derivation among the Yoruba. 'All the Orisa of Yorubaland are generally acknowledged to be in every case traceable to a human being.'[7] Mbiti also considers spirits in traditional religion to be created beings. 'Divinities are on the whole thought to have been created by God, in the ontological category of the spirits.'[8] Parrinder, an authority on West African religion, says: 'Any of the divinities worshipped in West Africa seem to have come from the personification of natural forces, since all the universe is thought to be peopled with spirits. Others are deified ancestors. Some may have a double quality, both human and divine combined.'[9] Indeed, it is difficult to see any clear difference between saying, with Idowu, that the divinities 'were brought into being' and saying that they were created.

Since the triune God alone is eternal, according to Scripture, it follows that in biblical perspective all divinities or spirits came into existence through the creative act of God. This is the truth about the origin of the spirit world. The Bible says of Christ,

> For by him all things were created, both in the heavens and on earth, visible and invisible, whether thrones or dominions or rulers or authorities all things have been created by Him and for Him. And he is before all things, and in Him all things hold together (Colossians 1:16,17).

Different types of spirits

Beliefs about the numbers, names, and orders of spirits vary among different African peoples. Certainly among the Yoruba the spirits are believed to be legion. Some speak of four hundred and others of six hundred. According to Gleason:

> Actually there are about forty active orisha in Yorubaland, and of these nine or ten are so important, so extensively

worshipped as to form a sort of pantheon, a set of the most powerful attributes of being.[10]

In general one may divide the spirit world of the Yoruba into four categories: (1) the primordial divinities, who existed before creation; (2) lesser divinities, principally historical figures who have been deified; (3) environmental spirits, personifying natural phenomena; and (4) ancestral spirits. Let me illustrate some of these.

Among both the primordial and lesser divinities of the Yoruba, the most widely known and worshipped would include the following. *Obatala* is considered the supreme divinity under God (Olorun), and indeed Olorun's vice-regent. He was God's agent in creation, and it is Obatala who is responsible for forming every human being coming into the world. *Orunmila* is looked upon as Obatala's deputy, acting often in a mediatorial role between the divinities and mankind. He is especially notable in 'matters pertaining to omniscience and wisdom,'[11] and therefore with oracles. As such, Orunmila is closely associated with *Ifa*, the spirit of divination, so much so that a distinction between the two is not always maintained. The name Ifa is used both for the oracular deity and for the complex oracular system associated with him. Because of his role, Ifa is a very popular deity in Yoruba traditional religion, and very widely worshipped. The Ifa cult is also highly organised with its own very successful priesthood. Thus it is said that 'Ebi ko le pa babalawo' (an Ifa priest can never starve).

Esu, 'the most ubiquitous of all orisa,'[12] is supposed to be worshipped in every traditional Yoruba household, with a representation of him sited just outside the household compound. Yoruba beliefs about the character of Esu are confusing. He is considered to be unpredictable, mischievous, deceptive, malevolent, and evil, and worshipped in fear. For this reason he has often been identified with Satan, the Evil One. This identification is denied by recent writers such as Parrinder and Idowu,[13] and Awolalu has written:

Esu is neither the devil of the Christian concept nor the Shaitan of the Muslim faith. The devil or Shaitan in these two religions is outright evil, but this is not so with Esu in Yoruba beliefs.[14]

The basis for such an affirmation is that, first, Yoruba religion is not dualistic; Esu is not taken to be in constant opposition to Olorun. Secondly, Esu is said to be a protector of his worshippers. And thirdly, he is a minister of Olorun to test and try people. Nevertheless, one cannot deny that many of the characteristics attributed to Esu are also attributed to Satan in the Bible. The biblical Satan undoubtedly protects his own, constantly tests and tempts, and is the father of lies. Like Esu, his worshippers only serve him in fear. Although the identification of the two may not be exact, so that Esu is not identical to 'the Evil One' of the Bible, nevertheless it can certainly be concluded that Esu is 'an evil one'. Writers who try to avoid this conclusion can only do so by ignoring the belief of the people.

Among well-known lesser divinities, *Ogun* is the Orisa of iron and of war, and hence the guardian of 'hunters, the blacksmiths, the goldsmiths, the barbers, the butchers and (in modern time) the mechanics, the lorry and taxi-drivers—indeed, all workers in iron and steel.'[15] *Sopono* is the spirit associated with smallpox. Because he is worshipped in fear, his shrines are found outside the town and in the bush. *Sango* is the Orisa of thunderstorms and lightning. *Orisa-Oko* is the divinity of the farm, agriculture, and harvest. He is especially worshipped with much festivity at harvest time.

The Yoruba also believe that spirits live in mountains, rivers, trees, and animals. Some are considered good, and some evil and dangerous. The Ogboni cult, for example, is focused on worship of the earth. In cities such as Ibadan the spirit of a prominent local hill is celebrated as protector of the community. Elsewhere Oya is worshipped as goddess of the River Niger.

Traditional religionists in many parts of Africa also attribute a prominent role to the ancestors in their religious beliefs and activities. When a Yoruba man is confronted with problems, he knows that his forefathers have had a similar experience. Hence he turns to them for help because he feels that his forefathers have more influence in affairs of this world. By worshipping the ancestors through libations and prayers, the Yoruba believe:

> that they are actively in touch with the spirit world, that the departed spirits of ancestors still take active interest in the affairs of their descendants, and that contact between the two can be very real, for good or ill. [16]

Yorubas like to acknowledge the presence of the ancestors through the Egungun cult. On important occasions, those from the community who are initiates of this cult will present themselves in elaborate costume representing the departed ancestors, and will parade the streets, dancing and receiving gifts from their admirers, or sometimes feigning hostility. Completely covered by their costume and often using masks, so that they cannot be identified as individuals, they are termed 'ara orun' (citizens of heaven), and are taken to be 'an embodiment of the spirit of a deceased person who returns from heaven to visit his people.'[17]

NOTES

[1] S.S. Farrow, *Faith, Fancies and Fetich*, 116.
[2] J.O. Awolalu, *Yoruba Beliefs*, 20.
[3] J.L. Nevius, *Demon Possession*, 245.
[4] E.B. Idowu, *African Traditional Religion*, 169.
[5] Ibid.
[6] Farrow, 34.
[7] Fadipe, 262.
[8] J.S. Mbiti, *African Religions and Philosophy*, 98.
[9] E.G. Parrinder, *West African Religion*, 26.
[10] J. Gleason, *Orisha*, 118-19.
[11] Idowu, *Olodumare*, 75.

[12] Fadipe, 285-86.
[13] Parrinder, 55-56; Idowu, *Olodumare*, 80.
[14] Awolalu, 28.
[15] Ibid., 31.
[16] Lucas, *The Religion of the Yorubas*, 119.
[17] Ibid., 137.

Chapter Five

Worship of the Spirits

Among most African traditionalists worship of the spirits takes place all day long. 'From dawn till dusk they offer ejaculatory prayers as occasion demands.'[1] For example, the Yoruba never leave their homes without first worshipping the spirit to which they are devoted, nor will they come across a shrine or symbol of their deity without a word of adoration and prayer. In addition each major spirit has a separate day of worship during the week. Hence Esu or Awo is worshipped the first day of the week, Obatala the second day, Oduduwa or Ogun the third, while Sango is worshipped on the fourth day.

Great annual festivals also honour the spirits, including sacrifices, dancing, spirit-possession, and much merry-making. Thus Awolalu writes: 'On joyful occasions, the people express gratitude to the divinities for protection, security and joy vouch-safed in the time past, and requests are made for the things desired.'[2] For example, at the annual Ogun festival, sacrifices are presented by the community with the following formula:

> Ogun, here are the festival kola nuts for you from all of us.
> Ogun, here is your festival snail from all of us.

> Ogun, here is your festival pigeon from all of us.
> Ogun here is your festival dog from all of us.
> Spare us so that we can do this again next year.
>
> Ward off death and sickness from us.
> Ward off accidents from us.
> Ward off untoward incidents from the young folk.
> Ward off untoward incidents from the elderly ones.
> Ward off untoward incidents from the children.
> Ward off untoward incidents from all pregnant women.[3]

Sacrifice to the spirits is indeed the centre of much African traditional worship [and will therefore be given particular attention later in this book]. Great significance is also attached to prayer. But, as in the example above, the contents of these prayers are usually materialistic, requesting various blessings and imploring protection from various dangers. Any sense of communion is largely absent. Idowu states that such prayers:

> consist usually of asking for protection from sicknesses and death, gifts of longevity, children, prosperity in enterprises, victory over enemies, protection from evil spirits and of relatives near and distant, rectification of unhappy destinies, and abundant provision of material things; blessing on all well-wishers and damnation on all ill-wishers.[4]

While most prayer will be directed to the spirits, among the Yoruba short prayers or acknowledgements will also be addressed to the Supreme Deity during the course of the day. For example: 'Olorun sanu' ('May God have mercy'), or 'Olorun gba mi' ('May God save me'). God's name is also invoked in greetings at the beginning of the day: 'E ka ro, Se e jire!' ('Good morning, I hope you wake up well!', to which the proper response is, 'A dupe lowo Olorun' ('Thanks be to God'). And the day is concluded with the saying: 'O da ro o, Ki Olorun ji wa re' ('Good night, may God wake us up well!'). While travelling, a Yoruba will greet with prayer, or when a baby is born a Yoruba will greet the parents with prayer in the name of God.

Praise songs addressed to the spirits are also very common in African traditional worship. 'The idea is that when the praise-names are given, or sung, the divinities will be moved to pay attention to the worshippers and thus heed their requests and wishes.'[5] Traditional rulers and well-to-do people are treated in the same way in ordinary life, so that the singers can entice money out of their pockets! Traditional religionists think that they can similarly move the spirits to respond to their requests with these praise songs. The Christians in Yorubaland have adopted this kind of praise song but with a different focus. The songs are now in praise to God for what He has already done through Christ.

Some spirits can be worshipped anywhere, but others can only be worshipped in the proper place. Among the Yoruba the first place for worship is the household spot marked out for worship of the spirits. The Yoruba houses are built in rectangular shapes with a large open space between the main building and the cooking area. In this space one usually finds a rectangular clay block about two feet wide on which is set the image of the family Orisa (spirit). Here offerings, such as palm oil or kola nut, are offered daily with prayers. In addition, shrines and temples are found everywhere, consisting for example of: 'small altars in the fields, forked posts in compounds, or large buildings in villages.'[6] Awolalu writes: 'Indeed there are as many shrines as there are divinities.'[7] Most shrines will be simple mud-walled buildings with thatched roofs. Inside the building may only be big enough to contain the objects of worship and space for the priest, but outside will be open space or courts for participants in the worship. At major centres, however, one will find substantial buildings, with trained priesthoods overseeing the worship. Traditional worship of the spirits may also be conducted at special places in the forest. Lucas writes:

> These are places where the thickness of the bush lends itself readily to the occult and sometimes nefarious practices carried on therein. . . . The sacred spot itself is marked by having one or more palm-fronds stretched across its entrance. The

palm-fronds serve as a sign to the uninitiated to avoid meddling with the grove, under pain of severe penalty. The palm-fronds . . . are regarded as effective jujus to such an extent that, although there are no human guardians on duty at the groves, the fear of the efficacy of the juju serves as an efficient check to the would-be intruders.[8]

The symbols of spirit worship may be made of wood or clay, and are intended to represent or illustrate a particular spirit. For example, among the Yoruba a common symbol representing Esu is a stone slab stuck slanting in the ground. While these objects may be used as aids to worship, they may frequently function much more as means of spiritual protection.[9] Parrinder reports:

I have seen a dozen or twenty separate pots and shrines at the house of a pious layman. Most family compounds have small mounds for one or more of the gods, some dishes by the house door for the twin cult and for Eshu, some iron rods (asen, osanyin) in a little hut for the ancestors, charms over the doorway and in the corners of the rooms, and a roughly carved 'guardian' post at the door fastened with a chain, to drive away and chain down evil.[10]

Christianity and spirit worship

Regarding the worship of spirits in traditional religion, Awolalu writes emphatically:

There is nothing wrong in employing different avenues of reaching the Supreme Being. The ancestors, divinities and spirits are means to an end; the end in view is Olodumare [God].[11]

But according to Scripture we are not left to choose for ourselves by what means we wish to approach God. Jesus said: 'I am the way, the truth and the life; no one comes to the Father but through Me' (John 14:6). According to biblical Christianity, any true and acceptable worship of God can only be done through Christ, who is the perfect sacrifice for the sin of the world. Any other forms of worship, no matter how organised, must be brought under the judgment of the Word of God. Praise and adoration according to the Bible are due to God alone. Since African traditional religion is found wanting in this regard, it is not acceptable.

But Christians need to know about traditional worship. We can learn from traditional worshippers. For example, as we have seen, they do not wait for Sunday to come before they worship their deities. They worship them at any time during the day, as well as weekly and annually. African Christians have something to learn from these non-Christians concerning priorities. The Bible admonishes Christians to pray without ceasing, but the traditionalists often put us to shame in this matter. African Christians also need to study traditional worship so that they can better witness to their non-Christian friends. We have noted that African traditionalists believe firmly in the efficacy of prayer. Since prayer is so important to them, the Christian is offered a workable tool for counselling and evangelism. For example, I once had the privilege of visiting a prominent Yoruba traditional ruler who was a Muslim. After discussion with him, I asked to take my leave, but the ruler challenged me with these words, 'Pastor, won't you pray for me?' I agreed, and immediately he knelt down, took off his hat (which is contrary to traditional custom), and I prayed for him in the name of Jesus Christ.

Monotheism or polytheism in African religion

The word 'worship' used in a religious sense refers to an active response of reverent devotion to God or to deities. Who does the African traditionalist worship, one God or many gods?

Idowu forcefully maintains that Yoruba religion is not polytheistic but modified monotheism. The modification is inevitable because of 'the presence of other divine beings within the structure of the religion.'[12] For Idowu, acts of worship addressed through intermediaries to the Supreme Deity are not incompatible with the nature of monotheism. To those, like Parrinder, who contend that West Africa exemplifies fully developed polytheism with its pantheons of nature gods, Idowu would answer that since these lesser gods were created by a Supreme Deity and derive all their powers from him, functioning as his intercessors and ministers, in worshipping them one is worshipping the One from whom they derive their origin and role. As such they are worshipped in a monotheistic context.

But those who adopt such a view cannot escape a pointed question. To whom is one to pay respect, to the One who sends the message or to the messenger? In order to worship the Supreme Being, does one have to worship divinities? In the end, the vital issue is not how we prefer to worship, nor whom we prefer to worship, but what God Himself has commanded us to do in His Word. And the Bible leaves no doubt at all on this matter. Paul wrote:

> Therefore, concerning the eating of things sacrificed to idols, we know that there is no such thing as an idol in the world, and that there is no God but one. For even if there are so-called gods whether in heaven or on earth, as indeed there are many gods and many lords, yet for us there is but one God, the Father, from whom are all things, and we exist for Him; and one Lord, Jesus Christ, by whom are all things, and we exist through Him (1 Corinthians 8:4-6).

In Biblical perspective, to worship divinities rather than the One God is polytheism, not modified monotheism. It is an unbiblical rationalisation to say of African traditionalists that 'they may appear to live their lives in absolute devotion to the divinities, but underneath all their acts of worship is the deep consciousness that Olodumare is above all and ultimately controls all issues.'[13] This is not the biblical perspective, and therefore cannot be acceptable to African Christianity. African traditionalists, in directing their worship to spirits, are worshipping only those spirits, and not worshipping the Creator God.

Christian worship of God

For biblical Christianity there is only one God, and the only true worship is that rendered to God and to God alone. As the Psalmist writes: 'Ascribe to the Lord, O families of the peoples, ascribe to the Lord glory and strength. Ascribe to the Lord the glory of His name' (Psalm 96:7-8). And the Apostle John writes: 'Worthy is the Lamb that was slain to receive power and riches and wisdom and might and honour and glory and blessing' (Revelation 5:12). Throughout the history of Israel, God's people are called to worship Him alone, and to forsake the gods of their neighbours. A man of God comes to Bethel to cry against the altar of Jeroboam (1 Kings 13). Ahijah the prophet pronounces judgment on Jeroboam for going after other gods (1 Kings 14). Elijah called on Israel to make their choice: 'How long will you hesitate between two opinions? If the Lord is God, follow Him, but if Baal, follow him' (1 Kings 18:21). Amos cries against the royal sanctuary at Bethel (Amos 5). Isaiah declares of Yahweh: 'I am the Lord, that is My name; I will not give My glory to another, nor My praise to graven images' (Isaiah 42:8) Hosea declares judgment on Ephraim because of her idolatry (Hosea 8). Jeremiah condemns the worship of the queen of heaven (Jeremiah 44).

Israel's sin is not that she totally rejected Yahweh but that she wanted to combine Yahweh worship with the worship of Baal. It is equally true today that while some Yoruba Christians worship God, they also worship different traditional divinities of the Yoruba. This is syncretism pure and simple. Idowu himself rightly says: 'We must admit that the danger of idolatry (properly defined) and syncretism is always with us.'[14] Indeed it is, if we worship anyone other than the one true God alone. Christ said to Satan: 'Begone Satan! for it is written, You shall worship the Lord your God and serve Him only' (Matthew 4:10).

And nowhere does the Word of God allow Christians to worship even the Lord God through images and idols. 'Not one complimentary word about the aesthetic or religious value of idols is found in the Bible,' writes George Peters.[15] The only descriptive words we find of idols are 'iniquity, vanity, nothingness, terror, abomination, labour, grief, horror, and the cause of trembling.'

Idowu laments, 'It is to be regretted, however, that the direct ritualistic worship of Olodumare as a regular thing is dying out in Yorubaland.'[16] It is to be regretted if the traditional worship is equal to, or superior to, biblical Christianity. But since it is not, if traditional worship is defective in Biblical perspective, then I must challenge my African brothers and sisters: 'How long will you hesitate between two opinions?' I can only agree with the conclusion Idowu gives in his study:

> A vacuum is being created with regard to religion in Yorubaland. And there are contending forces for the filling of the vacuum. Of all the forces at work, Christianity, by its unique and universal message, stands the best chance of fulfilling that which is implied in the Yoruba concept of God, and that for the benefit of the people of the country. This, however, depends as in every age and land upon the vision, spiritual stamina, and faithfulness of those who are charged with its message.[17]

In short, Africans worship the divinities and spirits because of their perceived functions, and in order to explain and cope with the problems of the environment. But in doing so, Africans are worshipping creatures rather than the Creator. Such worship is totally unbiblical and must be considered strictly unacceptable to Biblical Christianity on the continent.

The matter is not optional and not negotiable. God, and God alone, is to be worshipped and adored.

NOTES

1. S.S. Farrow, *Faith, Fancies and Fetich*, 39.
2. J.O. Awolalu, *Yoruba Beliefs*, 31.
3. S.A. Babalola, *The Content and Form of Yoruba Ijala*, 12-13.
4. E.B. Idowu, *Olodumare*, 116.
5. Awolalu, 103.
6. G. Parrinder, *West African Religion*, 61.
7. Awolalu, 114.
8. J O Lucas, *The Religion of the Yorubas*, 190-91.
9. Ibid., 190.
10. Parrinder, 61-62.
11. Awolalu, 67.
12. E.B. Idowu, *African Traditional Religion*, 168.
13. Idowu, *Olodumare*, 49.
14. E.B. Idowu, 'Introduction', in *Biblical Revelation and African Beliefs*, ed. by K.A. Dickson and P. Ellingworth, 11.
15. G.W. Peters, *A Biblical Theology of Missions*, 323.
16. Idowu, *Olodumare*, 143.
17. Ibid., 215.

Chapter Six

African Beliefs about Sacrifice

Sacrifice plays a central part in the traditional religion of Africa. In the relations mediated between man on the one hand and the world of God and the spirits on the other, sacrifice is a principal factor. When Africans first thought of offering sacrifices, where the idea came from, and who first instituted sacrifice is debatable. What can be said with certainty is that the sacrificial systems of Africa must stem from that consciousness common to all peoples that supernatural powers do exist, and that man is either in a good or a bad relationship with them. When in a good relationship, the offerer expresses gratitude to God, to the spirits, and probably to his ancestors, seeking favour from them all through gifts, offerings, communion and thank offerings. When the relationship is bad it is hoped through sacrifice to ward off evil and dangers. The main sources of information on this aspect of African religion, as on other aspects, are myths, liturgies, songs and sayings.

African sacrifice is similar to that of other nations. African sacrifice, like that of the Arabs, has more to do with major occasions in the life of individuals or communities than with great moral issues such as sin or restitution. Like the Egyptians, objects offered by the Africans in their ritual sacrifices included all kinds of domestic animals, birds, meal, wine and beer. Again, like the Egyptians, Africans not only offer sacrifices to the gods but also to the dead, to support them with food and drink, favour and fellowship. What is said by Steindorf regarding Egyptian ritual for the dead may also be said for Africa: 'The first duty of the relatives is, therefore, to see that the deceased lacks nothing'[1] And like the Canaanites of old, some African peoples traditionally sacrifice human beings in times of calamity.

The purposes of African sacrifice

One major purpose of African sacrifices is that by this means the offerers hope to obtain favour with the supernatural powers.

> They know that they depend upon these spiritual powers for material prosperity, for good health, increase in crops, in cattle and in the family. They therefore consider it expedient to show their gratitude for the good things received from them. Hence thank-offerings are made, especially on annual festive occasions.[2]

To seek favour from the gods, the offerer has to come before the specific deity, offering what the deity likes, and this must be done regularly. For example, at the time of the yam harvest, Yoruba people will first offer yams in a ceremonial manner to the divinities of the farm (especially the god of fertility) and to ancestral spirits. The belief is that these divinities and ancestral spirits made the crop yield well. Sometimes a sacrifice is offered at the graveside of a deceased father. Libations of wine and water are made, and kola nuts are offered (which may be shared among those present). The purpose is communion and fellowship with the living dead. As Awolalu writes, 'Here is an affirmation of the belief in the existence and power of the departed ancestors. As the living drink and eat together, so also, the invisible ancestral spirits, it is believed, will be well disposed to the living.'[3]

Thank offerings are undertaken to show appreciation to the divinities for success in any undertaking. 'Women who have sold well in the market, the person who has been blessed with a much-desired child, one who has received a special mark of divine favour, all want to show their thanks to the Orisa whom they believe to be the dispenser of their special blessing.'[4] A votive sacrifice conveys the idea of a covenant. A woman may promise to bring a gift of a goat or whatever else she can afford if she conceives a child. 'It is the strong belief of the Yoruba that whatever is vowed must be fulfilled on pain of serious consequences.'[5]

A second major purpose for sacrificing is to appease the spirits, to ward off evils and dangers, to forestall loss, sufferings, and accidents. Idowu writes of these as sacrifices of propitiation:

> Sacrifice in this category is known as Ebo-Etutu—'sacrifice of appeasement'. Usually, this sacrifice is prescribed by the oracle or an Orisa in reply to an enquiry as to what can be done to save this situation during a crisis like an epidemic, famine, drought or serious illness. In the olden days, a human offering used to be the main feature of the sacrifice.[6]

This type of sacrifice is never shared with the divinities. The material used in sacrifice is either burned, buried or treated with oil and exposed. Bus drivers usually kill dogs in sacrifice to Ogun, the god of iron, so that their buses may not be involved in accidents. Blood, oil, or food, is offered to ward off invisible spirits of evil. In such cases sacrifice is not for the sake of friendship, but to deflect the anger of spiritual powers and forestall any evil from their hand.

The contents of African sacrifice

The contents in African sacrifice vary from one circumstance to another and also from one divinity to another. While everything offered is something used by human beings in their daily life, the selection of what to offer in a particular case is governed by custom or by circumstance, or by oracle or diviner. For example, among the Yoruba the 'traditional tastes' of various Orisa are known.

> Ogun is very fond of dogs, palm wine, roasted yams, oil, snails, tortoises and, in some cases, rams. Orunmila loves rats and mudfish. Obatala is fond of snails fried in shea butter, cooked white maize, white kola nut or bitter kola.[7]

Whereas kola nut is a common offering, Obatala will not accept the red kola nut, since everything of a red colour is taboo for him. Only the white kola may be offered to him.

The animal or material used in sacrifice may have symbolic meanings. For example, since the sheep is a symbol for good health, diviners usually prescribe sheep for sacrifice against death in sickness. A dog is sacrificed for longevity. A ram and a cock are usually offered to obtain strength for the body. Another interesting symbol is that of the crab. If there is no rain, diviners may advise the heads of a city to sacrifice a male crab.

The supreme sacrifice of the Yoruba was human sacrifice. Human beings were sacrificed to the deities either to appease them or to carry the petitions of the community to the deities. In the former case, human beings were sacrificed during special national crises, such as death among the young men in the community, times of drought, a scourge of locusts, or an epidemic, since these crises were believed to be brought upon the community through the anger of the gods, for which a significant act of appeasement was required. In other situations the victim was seen as the representative of the people, being dispatched to carry their petitions to the higher power. In such instances the victim was accorded every honour, was well treated, well fed, and given every good thing he might ask for except his liberty and his life. 'Ironically enough, he was expected to put in every good word possible on behalf of those who offered him up.' [8]

While the Yoruba did offer victims from their own household, more often the victim would be a stranger, or perhaps a slave purchased from another village. Sometimes an oracle might be specific about the individual to be offered. In general the person was ritualistically beheaded and his body left exposed, or else he was buried alive, perhaps with only his head showing above ground. During the colonial period, human sacrifices among the Yoruba were made illegal. Certainly it is no longer a public affair, but whether such sacrifices continue to occur in Yoruba religion today cannot be determined. Idowu writes: 'No one can be quite sure that this sacrifice is not being offered, if secretly and only on urgent occasions even these days.' [9]

Those to whom African sacrifice is offered

Among most African peoples sacrifices are offered to the Supreme God only indirectly, never directly. For example, the Yoruba belief is that the spirits are all created by God, even the evil spirits, and these are agents or messengers of God. When sacrifice is offered to any of these subordinate spirits, the implicit concept is that they will take it to the Supreme God. Thus at any sacrifice the first response of the offerer is a prayer, 'May God accept the offering.' The final acceptance or rejection of the offering therefore lies with God, but God is not directly the object of the sacrifice.

Among the members of the spirit world to whom sacrifice is directed among the Yoruba, let me mention two in particular. One is Esu, who plays an important role in the process. Esu is often noted when sacrifices are offered to other gods. Known as the inspector-general, he is to be feared for he testifies to the acceptability of the sacrifice. A common saying is, 'When we offer sacrifice, we should set apart that of Esu.' Awolalu writes, 'Since Esu is believed to be a messenger not only to Olodumare but also to the divinities for good or evil, it may be said that he acts as an intermediary between man and the spirits to whom sacrifice is directed.'[10] But unlike that which is given to good spirits, what is offered is always something of little or no use for human life: 'strips of cloth, a lizard, a toad, rotten eggs, broken cowries, etc. The end is not to make friends with, but to drive away, the evil spirits.'[11]

The ancestors are also an important object of Yoruba sacrifice. Daily and annual sacrifices are also offered to ancestors, who are believed to be living after death and so in fellowship with the relatives who live on earth. Mbiti states, 'The departed, whether parents, brothers, sisters or children, form part of the family and must therefore be kept in touch with their surviving relatives. Libations and the giving of food to the departed are tokens of fellowship, hospitality and respect; the drink and food so given are symbols of family continuity and contact.' [12] The idea is that those who gives gifts to their ancestors may expect children who will in turn take care of them and remember them when they die.

NOTES

[1] G. Steindorf, *The Religion of the Ancient Egyptians*, 117.
[2] J.O. Awolalu, *Yoruba Beliefs*, 81.
[3] Ibid., 84.
[4] E.B. Idowu, *Olodumare*, 122.
[5] Ibid.
[6] Ibid., 123.
[7] Awolalu, 85.

8 Awolalu, 87.
9 Idowu, *Olodumare*, 119.
10 Awolalu, 92.
11 S.H. Ezeanya, 'God, Spirits and the Spirit World,' 44.
12 J.S. Mbiti, *African Religions and Philosophy*, 9.7.

Chapter Seven

Sacrifice in Biblical Perspective

A comparison of the concepts of sacrifice in African tradition and in the Bible is instructive. The sacrificial system of African traditional religion is similar in some ways to that practised by Israel in the Old Testament. But there are also important differences. And the approach of the New Testament to sacrifice stands in sharp contrast to the African traditional approach.

Comparisons between African and Israelite sacrifice

In comparing attitudes towards sacrifice evident in ancient Israel and in traditional Africa, we may first notice that both Israelites and Africans could look upon sacrifices as a means of obtaining favour. If engaging upon some enterprise such as a war or a hunting expedition, it was felt wise to sacrifice before the undertaking in order to secure assistance, and to sacrifice after the undertaking in order to express thanks. Among both peoples could be found a hope that by giving gifts the deity could be induced to render in return more than they had given.

Nevertheless, whatever some Israelites may have thought about sacrifice, the prophets of the Old Testament consistently pointed out that Israel did not receive blessings because of multitudinous sacrifices. According to Old Testament teaching, those who substituted sacrifice for genuine obedience to God were odious to Him. Only as the people obeyed the laws of God, so that their sacrifices became an outgrowth of their obedience, would God abundantly bless them (Malachi 3:10).

Both Israelites and traditional Africans also looked upon sacrifice as a means of fellowship and communion. As Idowu has stated: 'the offerings are means of communion between the Orisa and the worshippers who are his children, and consequently a means of fellowship among the children themselves.'[1] The African meal and drink offering has similarities with Israel's Passover, which was a meal of communion and fellowship between God and Israel. Oesterley notes that, 'Both in original and later times the Passover was a communion-sacrifice.'[2]

Africans believe that the spirit of the departed continues to abide for a certain period either in or near the body it has just left. Food and drink are offered to the departed spirit either for the purpose of communion or to prevent harm from the powerful spirit of the departed. It appears that some Israelites may have had a similar notion. Deuteronomy 26:14 gives the response of a godly Israelite to Yahweh, 'I have not eaten any of the sacred portion while I was in mourning, nor have I removed any of it while I was unclean, nor have I offered any of it to the dead.' The statement implies that there were some Israelites who sacrificed to the dead, but that the true follower of Yahweh certainly did not, for the statement continues, 'I have obeyed the Lord my God; I have done everything you commanded me.'

Blood sacrifice has two distinct features in African sacrifice. It creates a new bond among those who participate in the rite and, where deities or ancestors are worshipped, it is believed that the blood revitalises the ones to whom the offering is made. Sawyerr writes, 'Since blood is a gift, which is a vehicle of the life offered to another, it not only revives the life of the recipients, but it also gives new life to the donors.'[3] This must be seen as an important difference between African and Old Testament sacrifices. Biblical sacrifices were never a means of revitalising God or man. Yahweh forbade the Israelites to drink blood (e.g. Leviticus 3:17), whereas African priests and people participate in drinking blood. It could be that some Israelites had the idea, taken from surrounding religion, that Yahweh drank the blood of the sacrifice, but the Psalmist directly repudiates this idea about God. 'Do I eat the flesh of bulls, or drink the blood of goats?' (Psalm 50:13). To this rhetorical question the implicit answer is that such a thing is unthinkable. The act of pouring out the blood at the foot of the altar or sprinkling the altar with it symbolised rather that the victim's life was given to Yahweh.

As to the material content of the sacrifice, both ancient Israelites and traditional Africans utilise animals and food in their sacrificial offerings. But whereas Africans sometimes engaged in human sacrifice, and this was widely practised in the ancient world, Israelites were forbidden to do so (Leviticus 18.21; 20:2-5; Deuteronomy 12:31; 18:10).

The major distinction between African and Old Testament sacrifice, of course, concerns the one to whom the sacrifice is offered. Unlike African sacrifices, Old Testament sacrifices were offered directly to Yahweh and only to Yahweh. The Bible is very clear that any other practice has always stood under God's condemnation.

> You shall have no other gods besides me. You shall not make for yourself an idol in the form of anything in heaven above

or on earth beneath or in the waters below. You shall not bow down to them or worship them (Exodus 20:3-4).

Sacrifice in the New Testament

The New Testament takes the whole matter of sacrifice much further. The New Testament teaching on sacrifice is that Christ, the Son of God, has been made the final sacrifice for sin, once for all. Any further sacrifice, whether to spirits or even to God himself, is therefore to be eliminated.

The New Testament clearly teaches that the Old Testament sacrificial system was only foreshadow of the complete and perfect sacrifice which Christ made on the cross once for all. The Old Testament sacrifices pointed toward the true Sacrifice, but they were inadequate in themselves.

> The law is only a shadow of good things that are coming—not the realities themselves. For this reason it can never, by the same sacrifices repeated endlessly year after year make perfect those who draw near to worship. If it could, would they not have stopped being offered? For the worshippers would have been cleansed once for all, and would no longer have felt guilty for their sins. But those sacrifices are an annual reminder of sins, because it is impossible for the blood of bulls and goats to take away sins (Hebrews 10:1-4).

African traditional sacrifices as well are inadequate and done away with, and have no place in the new times that God has given us in Christ.

It is true that many professing Christians in Africa still offer sacrifices of different kinds to the spirits and ancestors. The simple explanation for this is that they are not deeply converted to Christianity, that they have neither understood nor appropriated what Christ has done on their behalf in his sacrificial death. They have yet to realise the full implications of this for their lives. Let us therefore take time to review these great implications of the sacrifice of Christ.

(1) *Christ's sacrifice atones for sin.* African sacrifices might be able to remove ceremonial pollution, like the breaking of taboos, but they are unable to remove the guilt of sin. They cannot provide inward cleansing. But according to the Bible, the blood of Christ powerfully atones for sin.

> The blood of goats and bulls and the ashes of a heifer sprinkled on those who are ceremonially unclean sanctify them so that they are outwardly clean. How much more, then, will the blood of Christ, who through the eternal Spirit offered himself unblemished to God, cleanse our consciences from acts that lead to death, so that we may serve the living God (Hebrews 9:13,14).

Why should Christ's blood have such power? First of all because, as the passage states, Christ offered himself. He chose to sacrifice himself. His sacrifice was rational, voluntary and spontaneous. 'It is not the slaughter of an unconscious, reluctant victim but an intelligent act of the highest spiritual obedience towards God (Philippians 2:8)', states Hewitt.[4] Furthermore, his blood was powerful because, as the passage states, Christ's offering was an unblemished offering. Both the African and the Levitical offerings may have been spotless outwardly, without external deformity. But only the offering of Christ was spotless throughout, not only outwardly but also inwardly. Christ can atone for sin because he himself was without sin.

(2) *Christ's sacrifice is substitutionary.* One purpose of African sacrifice is to offer an animal (or sometimes a human being) to take the place of another individual or a community. Hence, when a child is sick, a chicken or goat is killed, dressed with oil, and buried. The idea is that the victim has taken the place of the child, so that the child will not be killed by the disease. But in the sacrifice of Christ, the African is offered the perfect, complete substitution for those evils in his life far deeper than any physical disease. Christ takes those evils on Himself

in our place, for us, and on our behalf. 'For the Son of Man came not to be ministered to, but to minister and to give his life a ransom for many' (Matthew 20:28; Mark 10:45).

(3) *Christ's sacrifice made Him mediator of a new covenant.* The idea of a covenant is not foreign to traditional Africa. Covenants were made between two ethnic groups that they would not wage war against each other. This covenant was usually ratified with shedding of blood. There were covenants between individuals by which the thumb of each party was cut and each sucked the blood of the other. These acts established strong covenants in African religion and society. The Bible teaches that Christ's sacrificial death made him the Mediator of a new covenant, a new agreement between God and man, including the African.

> For this reason Christ is the mediator of a new covenant, that those who are called may receive the promised eternal inheritance—now that he has died as a ransom to set them free from the sins committed under the first covenant. . . . For a covenant is in force only when somebody has died (Hebrews 9:15-17).

As the passage states, the new covenant in Christ brings two benefits to those who accept Christ as their mediator with God. On the one hand they receive release and redemption from their sins, and on the other hand they receive the eternal inheritance which God has promised. Why then should African Christians continue with traditional sacrifices? These sacrifices involved covenants repeatedly made and broken, between man and man, and between men and spirits. But through the mediatorial death of Christ the African Christian has been granted once for all through an eternal covenant both complete redemption and also God's promised inheritance.

(4) *Christ's sacrifice destroys the power of the evil one.* It should be admitted that evil powers do exist, and that it is often through fear that Africans offer sacrifices to appease such powers. But Christ in his death on the cross has not only atoned

for sin, but he has also destroyed the power of the evil one over us.

> Since the children have flesh and blood, he too shared in their humanity so that by his death he might destroy him who holds the power of death—that is, the devil—and free those who all their lives were held in slavery by their fear of death (Hebrews 2:14-15).

Since Christ in his sacrificial death has overcome evil spiritual powers, the follower of Christ is delivered from the present tyranny of such powers. There is no need for African Christians to sacrifice anything to appease evil spirits; they need only to appropriate for themselves the sacrifice of Christ in order to experience freedom from the evil one.

(5) *Christ's sacrifice reconciles man to God.* African sacrifices are offered in part to appease the anger of the spirits. For example, if lightning strikes a house, a sacrifice is offered to the God of thunder to appease him. But man's problem is much deeper than such difficulties. Through his disobedience to God, man has become sinful. He has much more to be troubled about than appeasing mere spirits. Though he has known about God, he has not worshipped Him, but instead has worshipped created beings. This is as true of the African traditionalist as of any other peoples in the world. They have broken fellowship with their Creator. Instead of serving him, they have chosen to serve spirits which are creatures, thus making themselves the enemies of God.

> The wrath of God is being revealed from heaven against all the godlessness and wickedness of men who suppress the truth by their wickedness, since what may be known about God is plain to them, because God made it plain to them..., so that men are without excuse. For although they knew God, they neither glorified him as God nor gave thanks to him....: They exchanged the truth of God for a lie, and worshipped

and served created things rather than the Creator (Romans 1:18-20, 25).

Sacrifice to the spirits will not relieve man of God's just wrath. It is God with whom the African traditionalist and the African Christian must be reconciled, and for that problem traditional sacrifices will avail nothing.

But the good news of the gospel is that 'while we were yet sinners, Christ died for us' (Romans 5:8). God himself, through the sacrifice of Christ, has opened the way for reconciliation with Himself:

> All this is from God, who reconciled us to himself through Christ and gave us the ministry of reconciliation: that God was reconciling the world to himself in Christ, not counting men's sins against them. And he has committed to us the message of reconciliation. We are therefore Christ's ambassadors, as though God were making his appeal through us. We implore you on Christ's behalf: Be reconciled to God (2 Corinthians 5:18-21).

That indeed is the challenge of the Bible both to African traditionalists, and to any African Christians who have yet to take to themselves all that God has offered to them in the sacrifice of Christ. Christ's sacrifice is more than enough for all their needs.

Let me conclude with an abbreviated transcription of the early Yoruba Christian hymn, 'Jesu Olugbala mo f'ori fun'. The hymn is based on the Yoruba saying: 'I give my head to —', indicating the particular deity worshipped by the speaker. These early Yoruba Christians obviously understood something vital concerning the significance of Christ within their African context. This hymn is in fact their prayer—and a prayer still very relevant for those in the African context today who likewise wish to appropriate the sacrifice of Christ for themselves.

> Jesus Saviour, I give my head to you.
> O let me not perish, I pray.

He was very kind to me.
He came to earth for my sake.
He suffered for my sake.
He died for my sake.
He made propitiation for me.
He is interceding for me.

Jesus Saviour, I give my head to you.
O let me not perish, I pray.

Shango, Shango cannot save us.
Oya, Oya has no power.
Obatala did not create us.
Yemaja cannot give birth.
Every orisa is deaf.
Irunmale cannot save us.
God is ever kind.
He created us and He saves us.
Come let us serve God.
Cast away your orisas.

Jesus Saviour, I give my head to you,
O let me not perish, I pray.[5]

NOTES

[1] E.B. Idowu, *Olodumare*, 121.
[2] W.O.E. Oesterley, 106.
[3] H. Sawyerr, 'Sacrifice', 77.
[4] T. Hewitt, *The Epistle to the Hebrews*, 148.
[5] Adapted from *IWE ORIN MIMO FUN IJO ENIA OLORUN NI ILE YORUBA* (CSS Bookshops, 1978) 545-547.

Chapter Eight

Conclusion

It is commonly said that 'there is good in every religion.'[1] However, this recognition should not be taken to imply that all religions are equally good, or that every particular religion is entirely good.

It should be noted that there are good things in African traditional religion, which any Christian theology relevant to Africa must take into serious account. One example is the African belief in a Supreme Being. No matter how vague and imperfect their concept may be, yet their belief in God as the Creator and Supreme Ruler cannot be ignored. God did not leave himself without witness in Africa.

Furthermore, the African belief in the existence of spirits is in conformity with biblical teaching. Whatever the content of such beliefs, nevertheless the African belief in the reality of the supernatural realm must not be ignored. Indeed the African Christian has much to learn from the practices of African traditional religionists as they serve the spirits. Before any project is embarked upon, they will invoke the spirits to bless and help. Sacrifices are faithfully done and taboos carefully observed. All this stands as a challenge to African Christianity in its own patterns of worship.

Nevertheless, it must be concluded that there are recognisable defects in African traditional religion, when viewed from the perspective of Christian faith. First, general revelation, from which traditional religion has learned, cannot lead one to the experience of eternal salvation. Only through the special revelation of Christ in Scripture is such salvation available. The knowledge of God which the African traditionalist has cannot, and does not, bring one into close communion with the God of love and goodness.

Secondly, by worshipping the spirits, the African traditionalist has broken and disobeyed the law of God. No matter how cleverly the scholarly arguments may be devised, African traditional religion does worship by means of idols, which is condemned by God. It does worship spirits, which is also condemned. And while acknowledging the Creator, traditional religion is nevertheless polytheistic in practice, which is abhorrent to God.

Thirdly, the African sacrificial system, no matter what concepts are involved, is not adequate for the salvation of man. Effective reconciliation with God is only available through the sacrifice of Christ. This sacrifice provides all that man needs for good relations with God and with the world. No other sacrifice is needed, and no other is appropriate.

To whatever land or people it comes, biblical Christianity is unique, for it is built upon the solid rock which is Christ Jesus. Whatever the defects of those who brought Christianity to Africa, whatever the deficiencies of Christian practice in Africa today, the biblical message of Christianity remains true for Africa, as indeed it does for any part of the world: that Christ is the only way to God. As Jesus himself said: 'No one can come to the Father except by me' (John 14:6). This is the challenge—and the invitation—of Christian faith to traditional religion in Africa today.

NOTES

1 S.S. Farrow, *Faith, Fancies and Fetich*, 140.

BIBLIOGRAPHY

Adeyemo, Tokunboh. 'The Doctrine of God in African Traditional Religion.' Th.D. dissertation, Dallas Theological Seminary, 1978.

_____. *Salvation in African Tradition*. Nairobi: Evangel, 1979.

Arinze, Francis A. *Sacrifice in Ibo Religion*. Ibadan: Ibadan Univ Press, 1979.

Awolalu, J. Omosade. *Yoruba Beliefs and Sacrificial Rites*. London: Longman, 1979.

Babalola, S.A. *The Content and Form of Yoruba Ijala*. Oxford: Clarendon, 1966.

Bascom, William. *Ifa Divination: Communication between Gods and Men in West Africa*. Bloomington: Indiana Univ Press, 1969.

Biobaku, S.O. 'The Use and Interpretation of Myths' *Odu: Journal of Yoruba and Related Studies* 1 (1955) 12-17.

Chafer, Lewis Sperry. *Systematic Theology*. 8 vols. Dallas: Dallas Seminary Press, 1973.

Demarest, Bruce A. *General Revelation*. Grand Rapids: Zondervan, 1982.

Dickson, Kwesi and Ellingworth, Paul, eds. *Biblical Revelation and African Beliefs*. London: Lutterworth, 1969.

Ellis, A.B. *The Yoruba-Speaking Peoples of the Slave Coast of Africa*. London: Chapman & Hall, 1894.

Ezeanya, Stephen H. 'God, Spirits and the Spirit World,' in *Biblical Revelation and African Beliefs*, ed. by K. Dickson and P. Ellingworth. London: Lutterworth, 1969.

Fadipe, N.A. *The Sociology of the Yoruba*. Ibadan: Ibadan University Press, 1970.

Farrow, S.S. *Faith, Fancies and Fetich*. London: SPCK, 1924.

Frobenius, Leo. *The Voice of Africa*. 2 vols. London: Hutchinson, 1913.

Gleason, Judith. *Orisha: The Gods of Yorubaland*. New York: Atheneum, 1971.

Hewitt, Thomas. *The Epistle to the Hebrews: An Introduction and Commentary*. Grand Rapids: Eerdmans, 1960.

Idowu, E. Bolaji. *Olodumare: God in Yoruba Belief*. London: Longmans, 1962.

_____. *Towards an Indigenous Church*. Ibadan: Oxford University Press, 1965.

_____. 'God,' in *Biblical Revelation and African Beliefs*, ed. by K. Dickson and P. Ellingworth. London: Lutterworth, 1969.

_____. *African Traditional Religion: A Definition*. Maryknoll: Orbis, 1973.

Kato, Byang H. *Theological Pitfalls in Africa*. Nairobi: Evangel, 1975.

_____. *African Cultural Revolution and the Christian Faith*. Jos: Challenge, 1976.

Lloyd, P.C. 'Yoruba Myths—A Sociologist's Interpretation'. *Odu: Journal of Yoruba and Related Studies* 2 (1965) 20-28.

Lucas, J. Olumide. *The Religion of the Yorubas*. Lagos: CMS Bookshop, 1943.

Mbiti, John S. *African Religions and Philosophy*. New York: Doubleday, 1970.

_____. *Concepts of God in Africa*. New York: Praeger, 1970.

_____. *African Traditional Religion: An Introduction*. London: Heinemann, 1975.

Nevius, John L. *Demon Possession*. Grand Rapids: Kregel, 1963.

Oesterley, W.O.E. *Sacrifice in Ancient Israel*. London: Hodder, 1937.

Olowola, Cornelius A. 'The Concept of Sacrifice in Yoruba Religion.' Th.M. thesis, Dallas Theological Seminary, 1976.

_____. 'The Yoruba Traditional Religion—A Critique.' Th.D. dissertation, Dallas Theological Seminary, 1983.

Parrinder, Geoffrey. *West African Religion*. London: Epworth, 1961.

_____. *Religion in Africa*. Harmondsworth: Penguin, 1969.

Pascal, Blaise. *Pensées*. Baltimore: Penguin, 1966.

Peters, George W. *A Biblical Theology of Missions*. Chicago: Moody, 1972.

Ray, Benjamin C. *African Religions: Symbol, Ritual and Community*. Englewood Cliffs: Prentice-Hall, 1976.

Ryrie, Charles C. *A Survey of Bible Doctrine*. Chicago: Moody, 1972.

Sawyerr, Harry. 'Sacrifice,' in *Biblical Revelation and African Beliefs*, ed. by K. Dickson and P. Ellingworth. London: Lutterworth, 1969.

_____. *God: Ancestor or Creator*. London: Longman, 1970.

Smith, Edwin W., ed. *African Ideas of God*, 2nd ed. London: Edinburgh House Press, 1961.

Steindorf, George. *The Religion of the Ancient Egyptians*. New York: Knickerbocker, 1905.

Thiessen, H.C. *Lectures in Systematic Theology*. Grand Rapids: Eerdmans, 1949.

Warfield, Benjamin B. *The Inspiration and Authority of the Bible*. Grand Rapids: Baker, 1948.

ABOUT THE AUTHOR

The Revd. Dr Cornelius Abiodun Olowola is acting Provost of the ECWA Theological Seminary, Igbaja, Nigeria. A citizen of Nigeria, he took a BTh degree at Igbaja in 1973. He has also pastored churches in Ibadan and Egbe in Nigeria. After securing an MTh degree from Dallas Theological Seminary in the United States in 1977, he joined the faculty of ECWA Theological Seminary in Igbaja.

Dr Olowola's post-graduate research focused on African traditional religion. He is author of the book, *The Last Week: A Study of the Last Week of Jesus Christ on Earth* (Jos: Challenge Publications, 1988), and has also published articles in the *Africa Journal of Evangelical Theology*.

Dr Olowola has been Deputy Chairman of the Accrediting Council for Theological Education in Africa (ACTEA) since 1985. He recently spent a sabbatical teaching Bible and Missions at Bryan College in the United States. He and his wife Felicia are parents of two sons and two daughters.

www.ingramcontent.com/pod-product-compliance
Lightning Source LLC
Chambersburg PA
CBHW020359170426
43200CB00005B/229